The Passion Of Christ

Reflecting On History's Darkest Hour

Discovery Series Bible Study

No moments in history deserve more quiet reflection than the hours of Jesus' suffering just before His death. The angels of heaven must have gone silent as the Lord of the universe suffered in dimensions far greater than could ever be portrayed on any big screen or reenactment.

What happened in the dark shadows of gnarled and twisted olive trees can bring our hearts not only to sad wonder but to a lifetime of gratefulness.

In the following pages, RBC Senior Research Editor Herb Vander Lugt uses his lifetime of study and pastoral ministry to reflect on the meaning of what the world is once again recognizing as the passion of Christ.

Martin R. De Haan II, President of RBC Ministries

Publisher:	Discovery House Publishers
Managing Editor:	Bill Crowder
Editor:	Anne Cetas
Graphic Design:	Alex Soh, Ineke
Cover Photo:	Alex Soh © 2006 RBC Ministries
Study Guide:	Bill Crowder, Sim Kay Tee

This *Discovery Series Bible Study* is based on
"The Passion Of Christ: Reflecting On History's Darkest Hour" (Q0210),
one of the popular *Discovery Series* booklets from RBC Ministries.
With more than 180 titles on a variety of biblical and Christian-living issues,
these 32-page booklets offer a rich resource of insight
for your study of God's Word.
For a catalog of *Discovery Series* booklets, write to us at:
RBC Ministries, PO Box 2222, Grand Rapids, MI 49501-2222
Or, visit us on the Web at: www.discoveryseries.org

≋Discovery House Publishers

A member of the RBC Ministries family:
Our Daily Bread, Day of Discovery, RBC Radio, Discovery Series,
Discovery House Music, ChristianCourses.com

ISBN 978-1-57293-219-7

Table Of Contents

When Darkness Reigned

It is Thursday night in Israel. In a garden outside the city walls of Jerusalem, the full moon of Passover casts shadows among scarred and gnarled olive trees. Jesus has regained His composure after a period of intense emotional anguish. The glow of torches and the sound of many feet announce the appearance of Roman soldiers led by a group of religious leaders. They have come to arrest Jesus on charges of blasphemy. A man named Judas steps forward and identifies his friend and teacher with a kiss of betrayal. Jesus confirms, "I am He." At these words, the arresting group falls back. Jesus gently chides them, but allows them to take Him. As He does, He says, "But this is your hour—when darkness reigns" (Lk. 22:53).

**This was the beginning of history's darkest hour.
But in the darkness, God was at work.**

This arrest of Jesus marked the beginning of history's darkest hour. But in the darkness, God was at work.

Christ's Struggle In The Darkness

John Wesley said of Christ's followers, "Our people die well." Many do, even in the worst of times. History tells of men and women who remained serene, even joyful, while facing a martyr's death. Millions have calmly chosen torture and execution over disloyalty to their Savior. But for a period of time in the Garden of Gethsemane, Jesus did not show such composure. The Gospel accounts portray Him as deeply troubled and distressed on the eve of His trial and crucifixion. Asking Peter, James, and John to accompany Him and pray for Him, He separated Himself from them a short distance, fell to the ground, and prayed. But instead of remaining long in prayer as He had often done in the past, He soon returned to His disciples, apparently feeling a need for their companionship. He did this three times. According to the writer of Hebrews, "He offered up prayers and petitions with loud cries and tears" (5:7).

> **"He offered up prayers and petitions with loud cries and tears." —Hebrews 5:7**

There are those who have made an issue of Jesus' turmoil. Some have contrasted His anguish with the resolve of Socrates, who is said to have calmly obeyed the order to kill himself by drinking hemlock. They speak critically of Jesus' cry from the cross, "My God, My God, why have You forsaken Me?" (Mt. 27:46), saying it reflects devastating disillusionment and utter despair. But in their own darkness, many have closed their eyes to the significance of what transpired that night and on the day that followed. They have missed the fact that God and

Satan were, at this moment in time, engaged in the crucial battle in the War of the Ages.

> **Could we trust God even if He didn't answer our prayers for this one so dear to our hearts?**

In the following pages we will see how both God and Satan, together with the disciples and enemies of Jesus, were all contributors to the indescribable anguish Jesus endured that dark Thursday night and even darker "Good Friday."

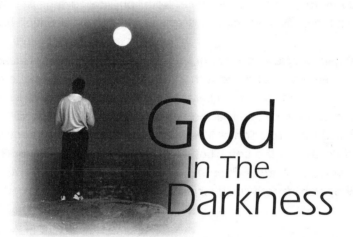

God
In The
Darkness

Loving fathers do all they can to protect their children from unnecessary pain. But according to the Bible, God the Father deliberately intensified the mental anguish and physical pain of His Son during the last 15 hours of His life. Isaiah 53:9-10, written some 700 years earlier, says, "He had done no violence, nor was any deceit in His mouth. Yet it was the Lord's will to crush Him and cause Him to suffer." About 25 years after the crucifixion of Jesus, the apostle Paul wrote, "God made Him who had no sin to be sin for us, so that in Him we might become the righteousness of God" (2 Cor. 5:21).

These are shocking words. Why would God intentionally "crush" His innocent Son? What did Paul mean when he said that God made "Him who had no sin to be sin for us"? To answer these questions, and to begin to understand the suffering of Gethsemane, we must look at the meaning of the word *death* in Romans 6:23, "For the wages of sin is death."

Seeing Our Need

As the "wages of sin," death involves more than the physical process of dying. The most important element in "death" as the "wages of sin" is spiritual rather than physical. To the people of Christ in Ephesus, Paul wrote, "As for you, you were dead in your transgressions and sins, in which you used to live" (Eph. 2:1-2). Notice that the Ephesians were "dead" while they were living. According to the Bible, every person before salvation is spiritually alienated from God. That is the reason for Paul's plea, "Be reconciled to God" (2 Cor. 5:20). To redeem us and make it possible for us to be spiritually alive—in touch with God—Jesus as our substitute had to experience both physical death (separation of the soul from the body) and spiritual death (separation or alienation from God).

When people reject the gospel, they remain spiritually dead. And when they enter eternity, alone and without Christ, they experience "the second death" (Rev. 20:14). This eternal separation from God forms the essence of hell. Therefore, when Paul said that God made Jesus "to be sin for us," he meant that God treated His sinless Son as if He were a sinner. He caused Jesus to experience physical death and the desolation of hell (the second death). In Galatians 3:13, Paul expressed this truth when he wrote, "Christ redeemed us from the curse of the law by becoming a curse for us, for it is written: 'Cursed is everyone who is hung on a tree.'"

Making A Sacrifice For Us

With this in mind, let's return to Gethsemane. We see Jesus "overwhelmed with sorrow to the point of death" (Mt. 26:38). Anguish swept over Him. He had often spent long evenings talking with and finding strength in His Father. But this night was different. Three times He got up to seek out His disciples. He was not finding satisfaction through prayer. Instead He sensed that His Father was beginning to withdraw from Him. This was the "cup" He dreaded (v.39). It would be so much easier for Him to suffer the physical pain associated with dying if He could do it while in communion with His Father.

Luke described only our Lord's third prayer, but he added a detail not mentioned elsewhere: "An angel from heaven appeared to Him and strengthened

Him. And being in anguish, He prayed more earnestly, and His sweat was like drops of blood falling to the ground" (Lk. 22:43). Notice that the coming of the angel both strengthened Him and increased His anguish. On the one hand, the angel apparently helped Jesus by assuring Him that, although the Father must withdraw His presence, the hosts of heaven were watching Him with breathless wonder. On the other hand, the coming of the angel increased His anguish, perhaps because it brought home to His soul the reality that God was indeed withdrawing from Him. Instead of speaking directly to Him, the Father spoke through one of His servants. Jesus was beginning to experience the desolation of hell.

> **It was necessary for the Son to face severe testing without sinning, and to suffer death in all its horror.**

Yes, He had chosen to undergo all the pain and shame that awaited Him without the help of His own divine power, without the comfort of the Holy Spirit, and without the support of His heavenly Father. Some 14 hours later, after almost 6 hours on the cross, the intensity of our Savior's spiritual anguish wrenched from Him the cry: "My God, My God, why have You forsaken Me?" (Mk. 15:34).

After receiving a drink of sour wine from a Roman soldier, Jesus realized that He had emptied the cup of God's wrath against sin. This brought a triumphant cry from His lips, "It is finished" (Jn. 19:30). All that was left for Him to do was die physically: "Father, into Your hands I commit My spirit" (Lk. 23:46). He bowed His head and gave up His spirit (Jn. 19:30).

As we reflect on this scene, we cannot help but think of the pain the Father and the Holy Spirit must have felt as they saw the Son, the fellow member of the eternal trinity, suffer and die as He did—abandoned and alone. How they must have longed to reach out, touch Him, and say, "We are here with You!" But to redeem us, it was necessary for the Son, who had become a member of the human family, to face severe testing without sinning, and to suffer death in all its horror. What incredible love!

STUDY
NO. *1*

Christ And God In The Darkness

Hebrews 5:7—"Who, in the days of His flesh, when He had offered up prayers and supplications, with vehement cries and tears to Him who was able to save Him from death, and was heard because of His godly fear."

Objective:
To see the work of God taking place in Gethsemane.

Bible Memorization:
Hebrews 5:7

Read:
"Christ's Struggle In The Darkness" and "God In The Darkness" pp.6-9

Warming Up

How do you feel when you are alone in dark places?
Does it bother you? Scare you? Excite you? Why?

Uneasy, fearful. Yes. Being alone in dark places causes a range of emotions. The uncertainty of being in the dark is what causes those emotions.

Thinking Through

On page 6, we read of those who contrast Jesus' turmoil at death with Socrates' "resolve." Do you think this is a fair comparison? What elements contribute to these events being so different? *No. Jesus' ~~chose~~ turmoil @ death was because of the separation from the Father. Also, He knew the process would be long + drawn out, lasting hours, horrific. Socrates' drinking of hemlock - Death probably came quickly*

In response to 2 Corinthians 5:21, we read (p.7), "These are shocking words. Why would God intentionally 'crush' His innocent Son?" What makes this idea so difficult to comprehend? What does it say about God's love for you? *It's difficult to comprehend because God is a God of Love; He is Love. He represents peace. The fact that He intentionally crushed His one + only Son—that I might be saved, demonstrates that He*

On page 9, Jesus' statement "It is finished" is described as "a triumphant cry." Why was it triumphant? How does that triumph impact us? *It's triumphant because it meant victory. He accomplished what He came to do. It impacts us in that we can know that in Jesus we have the victory also.*

Digging In

Key Text: Matthew 26:38-44

What did the "cup" represent? (v.39). Why would Jesus ask to be excused from taking it? *The cup represented suffering + separation from God. The thought of being separated from the Father @ such a crucial time, and during a most horrific experience caused Jesus agony*

10

What challenge did Jesus give to the sleeping disciples (see v.41), and why is it useful for us as well?

He told them to keep alert & pray. We must always be aware of the possibilities of temptation, its subtleties & stay spiritually fit to fight. Satan is very insidious & cunning

Jesus spent Himself in three sessions of prayer about the cup. Why was it necessary for Him to take the cup, in spite of the suffering it involved? *To accomplish our salvation.*

Going Further
Refer
Consider Hebrews 5:7 (this lesson's memory verse). How does it describe Christ's anguish in the garden? In what ways is this description similar to Matthew 26:38-44? In what ways are they different?

Christ's anguish in the garden was intense, as was His prayers.

Reflect
Have you ever pleaded with God to allow you to escape some coming difficulty? With what results?

Yes. Sometimes He did, sometimes He did not. It was all for my good. –Romans 8:28

How does the suffering of Christ in the garden speak to us in our suffering? What have you learned from the example of Jesus and His obedience? *We know that Jesus suffered greatly on our behalf, yet remained obedient to the Father's will. Obedience pays. No matter what God is always with us & rewards us for our obedience.*

[38]Then He said to them, "My soul is exceedingly sorrowful, even to death. Stay here and watch with Me." [39]He went a little farther and fell on His face, and prayed, saying, "O My Father, if it is possible, let this cup pass from Me; nevertheless, not as I will, but as You will." [40]Then He came to the disciples and found them sleeping, and said to Peter, "What? Could you not watch with Me one hour? [41]Watch and pray, lest you enter into temptation. The spirit indeed is willing, but the flesh is weak." [42]Again, a second time, He went away and prayed, saying, "O My Father, if this cup cannot pass away from Me unless I drink it, Your will be done." [43]And He came and found them asleep again, for their eyes were heavy. [44]So He left them, went away again, and prayed the third time, saying the same words. **Matthew 26:38-44**

Satan In The Darkness

God's archenemy also had a hand in the terrible suffering of Jesus in Gethsemane. Once the most exalted of God's created beings, Satan had led a rebellion against the God of heaven in prehistoric times. The Bible gives us no details, but the mysterious odes to the king of Babylon in Isaiah 14 and to the king of Tyre in Ezekiel 28 apparently contain allusions to the fall of the dark creature who was manipulating these kings for his own sinister purposes.

The prince of darkness undoubtedly hated Jesus because he knew the twofold purpose of Jesus' mission—to "save His people from their sins" (Mt. 1:21) and to "destroy the devil's work" (1 Jn. 3:8).

Seeing The Danger Of The Cross

I don't believe the devil and his demons rejoiced when Jesus was being nailed to the cross. They wanted Him dead, but not crucified. They knew that if Christ went to the cross He would pay the price for sin and break the power of death. The prince of darkness undoubtedly had a hand in King Herod's order to kill all the babies in Bethlehem (Mt. 2:16). It is possible that he also tried to kill Jesus in Gethsemane when His inner pain was so great that His "sweat was like drops of blood" (Lk. 22:44). But it appears that the enemy of God spent most of his energy in repeated attempts to keep Jesus from making a perfect sacrifice. This was clearly his aim when he and Jesus, by divine appointment, confronted each other in the wilderness. After describing the baptism of Jesus, Mark said, "At once the Spirit sent Him out into the desert, and He was in the desert forty days, being tempted by Satan" (Mk. 1:12-13).

Trying To Keep A Perfect Sacrifice From Being Made

The first temptation we are told about came after Jesus had been in the wilderness without food for 40 days. Knowing that Jesus was extremely hungry, Satan approached Him: "If [since] You are the Son of God, tell these stones to become bread" (Mt. 4:3). He urged Jesus to exercise His own power without regard to the Father's will. Jesus replied by quoting Deuteronomy 8:3, "Man does not live on bread alone but on every word that comes from the mouth of the Lord."

In Deuteronomy, Moses was reminding the Israelites that God humbled them by making it necessary to live on manna instead of on food they provided for themselves. He did this to teach them to rely on God rather than on their own efforts. Jesus saw His hunger as appointed by His Father, so He wouldn't satisfy His hunger by taking matters into His own hands. He had laid aside the independent exercise of His power as God so that He could live as a frail human. He did this so that He could experience the testings of life just as we do. He chose to depend on God just as we must. He refused to violate this commitment by miraculously satisfying His hunger.

Jesus chose to depend on God just as we must.

Satan's second effort to abort Christ's mission was less subtle. Either supernaturally or in a vision, the devil took Jesus to the highest spot of the temple complex, perhaps where it overhung the Kidron Valley. He suggested that Jesus jump—a drop of some 450 feet—reminding Him of Psalm 91:10-12, "He will command His angels concerning you . . . so that you will not strike your foot against a stone." Satan may have been suggesting that the sight of angels rescuing Jesus from certain death would so impress the masses around the temple that they would instantly accept Him as their promised Messiah. But Jesus responded by quoting Deuteronomy 6:16, "Do not test the Lord your God."

The devil's third attempt to keep Jesus from the cross was more direct. It was brash and bold. From a high mountain (again, either by his supernatural power to transport or in a vision), the devil showed Jesus all the kingdoms of the world, saying that he would relinquish his claim to them on one condition—that Jesus kneel before him in worship. He was implying that the end justifies the means.

Just one act of worship, and Jesus could achieve His goal—to wrest from Satan all the kingdoms over which he now ruled as "the prince" (Jn. 12:31; 14:30; 16:11). Jesus did not contest his claim, but He flatly rejected the offer. He knew that evil can never be overcome with evil. He sent the devil away by again quoting the Scriptures: "Worship the Lord your God and serve Him only" (Lk. 4:8; cp. Dt. 6:13).

> **Peter was horrified. How could the living God let this happen to His sinless Son?**

Luke said, "When the devil had finished all this tempting, he left Him until an opportune time" (4:13). The devil had been thoroughly defeated, so he left Jesus—for the moment. But he undoubtedly tried, whenever he saw an opportunity, to persuade Jesus that He could gain His objective without going to the cross.

Speaking Through Jesus' Close Friend

Matthew 16:13-28 records a conversation that describes an attempt by Satan to influence Christ through the words of a close friend. It happened toward the end of Jesus' 3 years of public life. Peter, a faithful disciple, had just made the great confession, "You are the Christ, the Son of the living God" (v.16). Jesus had commended him. But when He "began to explain to His disciples that He must go to Jerusalem and suffer many things . . . , and that He must be killed and on the third day be raised to life" (v.21), Peter was horrified. How could the living God let this happen to His sinless Son? So Peter "took [Jesus] aside and began to rebuke Him. 'Never, Lord!' he said, 'This shall never happen to You!'" (v.22).

I'm sure that Peter meant well. He loved Jesus. He believed his Teacher was the promised Messiah-King who would soon establish His kingdom on earth. So he must have been surprised by Christ's severe response: "Get behind Me, Satan! You are a stumbling block to Me; you do not have in mind the things of God, but the things of men" (v.23). How different from just a few moments before! Instead of commending him, Jesus severely rebuked him, even addressing him as "Satan." Peter had unwittingly become a tool of the devil to do his best to dissuade Jesus from going to the cross.

Waging The War Of The Ages

Jesus' life on earth, from His birth to His death on the cross, was a battle with the devil—the decisive battle in the War of the Ages. Keep in mind that one of the prime objectives in Christ's coming was "to destroy the devil's work" (1 Jn. 3:8). And Jesus didn't underestimate His enemy. Three times during the last week of His earthly life, Jesus referred to Satan as "the prince of this world" (Jn. 12:31; 14:30; 16:11). The word He used (archon) was often employed to denote the highest official in a territory or nation. Jesus knew He had engaged the undisputed head of a vast army of fallen spirits. Satan was the leader of the kingdom of evil that is the very antithesis of the kingdom of God. He and his demons had turned the good creation that came from the hand of God into a sin-infested, crazy world. Because of him, the world today is a place where natural disasters can kill thousands of innocent children while leaving thousands of scoundrels untouched. It is a world in which the lives of decent people are often filled with pain and disappointment while those of villains are marked by health and success. It is a world where good people are often the victims of rogues. All this is because Satan is now the "god of this age" (2 Cor. 4:4).

The enormity of Jesus' suffering in Gethsemane, therefore, represents a "war of the gods." Jesus had come to "destroy the devil's work," and His agony in the garden represented a crucial and decisive phase of His battle with the "prince of darkness."

> **The enormity of Jesus' suffering in Gethsemane represents a "war of the gods."**

By His birth into this world, the Lord of lords had entered territory that the devil and his armies were occupying. The apostle John wrote, "The whole world is under the control of the evil one" (1 Jn. 5:19). In the hills of Galilee, in the streets of Jerusalem, and finally among the olive trees of Gethsemane, the King of kings took on all the hosts of evil.

Along the way, there were those who tried to place Christ on the other side of this battle. Yet, when someone accused Him of casting out demons by the power of Beelzebub, He replied, "If Satan drives out Satan, he is divided against himself. How then can his kingdom stand? . . . But if I drive out demons by the Spirit of God, then the kingdom of God has come upon you. Or again, how can anyone enter a strong man's house and carry off his possessions unless he first ties up the strong man?" (Mt. 12:26-29).

In tying up "the strong man" (Satan), Jesus exercised His authority over Satan and his realm. By suffering in Gethsemane and dying on the cross, Christ gave us a basis for praying, "Your kingdom come, Your will be done on earth as it is in heaven" (Mt. 6:10).

By healing the sick, casting out demons, and raising the dead, Jesus entered Satan's realm and showed His mastery over all the forces of evil. Through His death on the cross and His resurrection, He would bind the enemy. The devil knew this. So he intensified his opposition to Jesus as the fateful hour drew near. He may have had a role in bringing into the heart of Jesus a deep sense of dread during the last week of His earthly ministry. This feeling of dread led Him to exclaim: "Now My heart is troubled, and what shall I say? 'Father, save Me from this hour'? No, it was for this very reason I came to this hour. Father, glorify Your name!" (Jn. 12:27-28).

Through His death on the cross and His resurrection, He would bind the enemy.

Because He had set aside the independent exercise of His divine attributes, Jesus was subject to feelings of dismay just as we are. But as much as He dreaded taking the curse of sin upon Himself, He rejected any thought of turning back. Yet He needed a word from His Father at this moment. So after His petition, "Father, glorify Your name," His Father graciously responded with a voice from heaven, "I have glorified it, and will glorify it again" (v.28). At this, Jesus said triumphantly, "Now is the time for judgment on this world; now the prince of this world will be driven out" (v.31).

What did Jesus mean when He used the word *now* to describe the defeat of Satan? It appears that His agony in Gethsemane and His suffering on the cross didn't overthrow the enemy. Satan was still active 20 years later when the apostle

Paul called him "the god of this age" (2 Cor. 4:4). And 15 years later, Satan was still a menacing figure, for the apostle Peter said that he "prowls around like a roaring lion looking for someone to devour" (1 Pet. 5:8). Thirty years after Peter wrote his letters, the apostle John declared that the "whole world is under the control of the evil one" (1 Jn. 5:19). Obviously, Satan has not yet been "driven out" from the earth. He is still a powerful adversary. But Jesus was not mistaken. Through His suffering and death, He dealt the death blow to Satan and his followers. By His resurrection, He served notice that their doom is sure. They know that when Jesus said "It is finished" and breathed His last, He had paid the full price for the sins of the whole world. That's why the demons "shudder" when they think about God (Jas. 2:19).

Satan has no power to bring eternal harm to those who are in Christ.

Satan has no power to bring eternal harm to those who are in Christ. This fact led Paul to write, "When you were dead in your sins . . . , God made you alive with Christ. He forgave us all our sins, having canceled the written code . . . that was against us . . . ; He took it away, nailing it to the cross. And having disarmed the powers and authorities, He made a public spectacle of them, triumphing over them by the cross" (Col. 2:13-15).

Paul portrayed Jesus ascending as a mighty conqueror, like a victorious general publicly displaying his victory over his enemies by leading them through the streets of a city, disarmed and shackled. Satan has been defeated, put to shame, and disarmed by Christ's cross and all that followed. The reality of this victory has not yet been fully realized. That awaits a later day. But the forces of darkness know that the day is coming when death will be "swallowed up in victory" (1 Cor. 15:54), and they will be "thrown into the lake of burning sulfur" (Rev. 20:10). No wonder Satan did all he could to keep Jesus from meeting His appointment with death on a cross.

STUDY NO. 2

Satan In The Darkness

Objective:
To see how Satan was at work in the events of Gethsemane.

Bible Memorization:
1 Corinthians 15:54

Read:
"Satan In The Darkness" pp.12-17

Warming Up
We live in a world that is often (if not always) at war somewhere. Why do you think such conflict exists? When can it be a good thing? When bad?

Thinking Through
On page 12, we are told of Christ's twofold purpose for His death. What were those two purposes, and how did He accomplish them?

Satan's attempts to disrupt Christ's mission fall into three categories (pp.13-14). What were those efforts, and how did Jesus respond to each of them?

"Jesus' life on earth, from His birth to His death on the cross, was a battle with the devil—the decisive battle in the War of the Ages" (see p.15). Why is Satan at war with God? What are some evidences of the ongoing conflict between God and Satan?

Digging In
Key Text: Colossians 2:13-15
What act of Christ (v.13) moves the child of God from being "dead in . . . trespasses" to being "made alive together with Him"?

How (v.14) did Jesus deal with the charges that were written against us?

What does it mean when Paul says that Jesus "disarmed principalities and powers"? (v.15). What constituted His triumph over them?

Going Further
Refer
In 1 Peter 5:8-9, we see the ongoing pressure and presence of our spiritual enemy, the devil. Since Christ defeated him, how does his influence still continue?

What verbs does Peter use to describe our stand against Satan? How did Christ practice those actions in the garden?

Reflect
How does it make you feel to know that Jesus has assured us spiritual victory through His triumph? How can you more intentionally live in that hope and confidence?

[13]And you, being dead in your trespasses and the uncircumcision of your flesh, He has made alive together with Him, having forgiven you all trespasses, [14]having wiped out the handwriting of requirements that was against us, which was contrary to us. And He has taken it out of the way, having nailed it to the cross. [15]Having disarmed principalities and powers, He made a public spectacle of them, triumphing over them in it.
Colossians 2:13-15

[8]Be sober, be vigilant; because your adversary the devil walks about like a roaring lion, seeking whom he may devour. [9]Resist him, steadfast in the faith, knowing that the same sufferings are experienced by your brotherhood in the world.
1 Peter 5:8-9

Christ's Disciples In The Darkness

It's important for us to take a closer look at how 12 of our Lord's closest followers unwittingly became the instruments of Satan in his battle against Jesus. It seems that Satan had at least two objectives in working through the friends of Jesus. First, he desperately wanted to convince Jesus that human beings are not worthy of all He had in mind to do for them. Second, he hated the Savior so much that even if he failed to accomplish this goal, he could add to the pain and shame of His journey to the cross.

We must keep in mind that it was through His death, not through the physical and psychological suffering that preceded it, that He paid the price for sin. God was not and is not a shylock demanding from Jesus a pound-for-pound amount of pain that we deserve because of our sins. The suffering and shame Jesus experienced on the way to His death came about because God allowed the devil to do his utmost to harm Jesus and win his battle against the Son of God. This fact accounts for the statement Jesus had made to the arresting party in Gethsemane: "But this is your hour—when darkness reigns" (Lk. 22:53). We will trace the events in this part of the story in their chronological order.

The Apathy Of Peter, James, And John

Jesus entered the Garden of Gethsemane an hour or so before midnight. He told eight of His disciples to sit down and pray. Then He took Peter, James, and John with Him a bit farther into the garden and said, "Stay here and keep watch with Me" (Mt. 26:38). He walked a short distance from them, fell to the ground, prayed, returned to the three, and found them asleep. One can feel His hurt in His words: "Could you men not keep watch with Me for one hour? . . . Watch and pray so that you will not fall into temptation" (vv.40-41). He knew they would soon be tempted to forsake Him and flee.

The fact that He repeated the sequence three times—praying, returning to His disciples, and speaking to them—clearly indicates that something unusual was going on. Normally He could spend hours in communion with His Father, but now He yearned for the companionship of the disciples. The best explanation seems to be that He sensed the beginning of His Father's withdrawal from Him. Jesus, having set aside His glory as God to become one of us, was deeply troubled by the realization that He would have to go on alone. He had to face all that awaited Him with the same emotional make-up, the same bodily structure, and the same vulnerability to pain that we have when we face our lesser trials.

The disciples' lack of genuine sympathy added to our Savior's anguish.

The sleeping on the part of the disciples might be understandable to us. It's true that they had gone through an extremely exhausting day. Yes, it was nearly midnight and they were sleepy. But they must have known something unusual and terrible was happening. Their Teacher was in agony. It's expected that friends will stand by one another when they know they are needed. The disciples' lack of genuine sympathy added to our Savior's anguish.

The Treachery Of Judas

The name Judas Iscariot is synonymous with treachery. He is the disciple who led the enemies of Jesus to Him, identifying Him with a kiss. Because Jesus had chosen him as one of the Twelve, He must have seen in him qualities that were consistent with the other disciples. Jesus had honored him by making him treasurer of the small band. He had included Judas with the others as one of the Twelve when He sent them out with "authority to drive out evil spirits and to heal every disease and sickness" (Mt. 10:1). But this man who seemed to have such potential for service in Christ's kingdom became a willing instrument of the enemy.

When Judas saw that Jesus was not ready to set up the long-awaited kingdom, he apparently became embittered and started stealing from the disciples' "money bag" (Jn. 12:6). Jesus knew what Judas was doing and was already aware of the betrayal he was planning, long before he carried it out. Earlier, Jesus had called Judas a "devil" (Jn. 6:70). But He did so in a manner that did not let the others know to whom He was referring.

Early in the evening of that last Thursday, Jesus clearly declared that one of the Twelve was about to betray Him. He said this betrayer would do to Him what a close companion did to David long ago, quoting Psalm 41:9. "He who shares My bread has lifted up his heel against Me" (Jn. 13:18).

Later that evening, when Jesus celebrated the Passover with the apostles, He gave Judas the place of honor on His left, with John on His right. This explains why He could converse with these two and not be overheard by the rest of the Twelve.

Shortly after they began eating, Jesus identified the traitor to John alone by dipping a morsel in the dish and giving it to Judas. This courtesy was normally perceived as a gesture of love reserved for someone special. I believe it was a loving appeal by Jesus—a tender plea to repent.

Judas was not an innocent victim of God's preordained decree.

A surge of emotion must have swept over Judas at that moment, but he had so hardened his heart that he could resist all his better instincts and carry out the evil that was in his heart. It was only after Judas had left the upper room and reached the point of no return that Jesus referred to him as the man "doomed to destruction" (Jn. 17:12).

Judas was not an innocent victim of God's preordained decree. He was responsible for his own decisions. He could have acted differently. If he had responded to Jesus' veiled warnings with a change of heart, the words of David in Psalm 41:9 would have applied only to the king's own experience. It would have had no further application.

In considering Jesus' prediction that one of the Twelve would betray Him, we must keep in mind that such announcements about the future were often open-ended. For example, on orders from God, Jonah proclaimed to the people of Nineveh, "Forty more days and Nineveh will be overturned" (Jon. 3:4). According to the record, that is all Jonah said. He made no call for them to repent and he promised no mercy if they did. Yet "when God saw what they did and how they turned from their evil ways, He had compassion and did not bring upon them the destruction He had threatened" (v.10).

The experience of Hezekiah offers another such example. Isaiah said to him: "This is what the Lord says: 'Put your house in order, because you are going to die; you will not recover'" (2 Ki. 20:1). He gave no indication that this declaration was conditional. But when the king prayed and wept, the Lord stopped the prophet before he had left the palace, telling him to go back to the king with the good news that He had heard his prayer and would give him a 15-year extension of his life (vv.5-6).

> **God doesn't make anyone a helpless pawn
> on the chessboard of fate.**

Such God-given announcements in the Bible are warnings of what will take place if the individuals or nations addressed continue on their present course. God sees the heart, and knows what is there when the warning is given. If He sees a change of heart, He cancels the warning. God's foreknowledge is not in question. God knew what was in the heart of Judas, and knew what he was going to do. But this foreknowledge put no constraint on Judas. Had he changed his mind, confessed his sin, and sought forgiveness, God would have foreknown that too. He would have allowed Judas to continue and become one of the pillars in the church. That is God's way of working. He doesn't make anyone a helpless pawn on the chessboard of fate. On the contrary, "He is patient . . . , not wanting anyone to perish, but everyone to come to repentance" (2 Pet. 3:9).

As we have already seen, this interaction of divine will and human will was true even in Old Testament times. Through His prophet Jeremiah the Lord had said, "If at any time I announce that a nation or kingdom is to be uprooted, torn down, and destroyed, and if that nation I warned repents of its evil, then I will relent and not inflict on it the disaster I had planned" (Jer. 18:7-8). The fact that Judas became a man "doomed to destruction" was not God's doing. This fate was of the disciple's own making.

We should also be careful not to overlook the pivotal role that Satan played in this sad scenario. Earlier we pointed out that Jesus' dipping the bread in the dish and giving it to Judas was a mark of special honor. The apostle John said that it was at this very moment that "Satan entered into him" (Jn. 13:27). The devil was able to do this because Judas had already opened the door to him by plotting the betrayal of Jesus. He undoubtedly strengthened Judas' resolve. Satan may have hoped that this terrible act by one of Jesus' own disciples would so crush His spirit that He might decide that people are not worth the price He would need to pay for their redemption.

One thing is sure: Satan knew that the dark betrayal of a friend would add to the burden of pain already on Jesus' shoulders. To be betrayed by someone you love and trust, someone with whom you have shared secrets, is one of life's deepest hurts. You can feel the pulse of sorrow in the words of David: "Even my close friend, whom I trusted, he who shared my bread, has lifted up his heel against me" (Ps. 41:9). This was Satan's hour. If he could not dissuade Christ from going to the cross, he could at least contribute to the Savior's pain and shame.

The Fear Of All The Disciples

Something else that added to Jesus' pain was that all of His friends would abandon Him. According to Matthew, when Jesus was arrested in Gethsemane, "all the disciples deserted Him and fled" (26:56). Jesus had warned them while on the way from the upper room to Gethsemane: "This very night you will all fall away on account of Me" (v.31). Instead of responding to this warning with humility, Peter was brash and self-confident. He boldly declared that he was ready to stand with Jesus, even to die with Him. "And all the other disciples said the same" (v.35). But "all the disciples deserted Him and fled" (v.56).

Think of how Jesus felt as they abandoned Him at the very moment His human heart so longed for their support and encouragement! Just a few moments before, while He was praying, He sensed that His Father was withdrawing from Him. God had to do this so that Jesus might become "sin for us" (2 Cor. 5:21). Now

25

with the disciples gone, Jesus was bereft of even human companionship.

I recall vividly an incident that showed me how much human companionship can mean when one faces death. I had spent time talking and praying with an elderly bachelor and was about to leave the room. I intended to return, knowing that he had no family. But with his finger he beckoned me to return to his side. He did not want to be alone. I could not leave him, not even for a few minutes. He became peaceful and very quickly fell asleep in Jesus.

> **To sense another person's presence while facing death is a strong human need.**

To sense another person's presence while facing death is a strong human need. But Jesus now saw that during the terrible hours ahead, until He would breathe His last, He would be alone—with neither His Father nor His disciples at His side. This was Satan's way of adding another weight to our Savior's burden of pain and sorrow.

The Denials Of Peter

Peter, the disciple who at Caesarea Philippi had so nobly confessed that Jesus was "the Christ, the Son of the living God" (Mt. 16:16), added still another weight to the Savior's suffering. Earlier, when Peter had so brashly declared his courage, Jesus had warned him: "I tell you the truth, . . . today—yes, tonight—before the rooster crows twice you yourself will disown Me three times" (Mk. 14:30). In spite of his bravado, he, like the rest of the disciples, had fled when Jesus was arrested. Yet Peter could not abandon Jesus completely. Keeping a safe distance so that he wouldn't be identified as a disciple of Jesus, he followed the arresting party "right into the courtyard of the high priest" (v.54).

Here again he tried to hide his identity. But it seems that he must have looked out of place among the enemies of Jesus. Three times in rapid succession he was confronted by someone accusing him of being one of the Lord's followers. Each time, he denied any relationship to Jesus. The third time, "he began to call down curses on himself, and he swore to them, 'I don't know this man you're talking about'" (v.71).

26

Luke completed the story: "Just as he was speaking, the rooster crowed. The Lord turned and looked straight at Peter. Then Peter remembered the word the Lord had spoken to him . . . . And he went outside and wept bitterly" (Lk. 22:60-62).

I have often wondered what Peter saw in the eyes of Jesus. I'm sure he did not see icy anger or cold disdain. He may have seen a look of disappointment. But above all, I believe he saw an abyss of hurt and oceans of love in the eyes of Jesus. This broke Peter's heart and led to bitter weeping.

Luke said that when Jesus had forewarned His self-confident friend about these upcoming denials, He had begun by saying, "Simon, Simon, Satan has asked to sift you as wheat. But I have prayed for you, Simon, that your faith may not fail" (22:31). And because this was the hour "when darkness reigns" (v.53), the devil was permitted a free hand. Peter's courage failed and he did what he never dreamed he would do. But the prayer of Jesus was answered—Peter's faith did not fail. He never quit believing in Jesus as the Messiah, the Son of God. He repented and later was publicly restored (Jn. 21:15-19). The test Satan had in mind for Peter would be intense—like the vigorous shaking of wheat in a sieve to separate the kernels from the chaff.

> **The test Satan had in mind for Peter would be intense— like the vigorous shaking of wheat in a sieve to separate the kernels from the chaff.**

Peter went on to become the fearless and powerful preacher on the Day of Pentecost, the day the church was born (Acts 2:1-41). He became the recognized leader in the apostolic ministry to the Jews. He wrote two letters that have been incorporated in the New Testament Scriptures. He endured fierce persecutions for his faith and he died a martyr. The devil had succeeded in making him an instrument to intensify Christ's sorrow and pain on the road to Calvary, but he had not been able to destroy him.

STUDY
NO. 3

Christ's Disciples In The Darkness

2 Corinthians 5:21—"He made Him who knew no sin to be sin for us, that we might become the righteousness of God in Him."

Objective:
To see how Jesus' followers responded to the challenge of Gethsemane.

Bible Memorization:
2 Corinthians 5:21

Read:
"Christ's Disciples In The Darkness"
pp.21-27

Warming Up
Have you ever failed in an opportunity to represent Christ? What were the circumstances, and how did you feel about that failure afterward?

Thinking Through
On pages 21-22, we read about the apathy of Jesus' three key disciples. What portrays that apathy to us, and how did it set up Peter for his denials of Christ?

Judas' involvement in Jesus' last days is described with the word *treachery* (pp.22-25). What did Judas know about Jesus and His character that made his rejection such a tragedy?

All of Jesus' disciples are seen as responding with fear (pp.25-26). What makes this response reasonable? What might make it inappropriate?

Digging In
Key Text: John 21:15-18
In our key text, we consider the restoration of Peter following his denials. Why did Jesus question Peter three times about the genuineness of his love?

What task did Jesus assign to Peter in order to tangibly demonstrate the character of his love? Who would Peter be working with?

How did Jesus describe Peter's end in verse 18? How might that have actually been encouraging to the once-failing disciple?

Going Further
Refer
From this lesson's memory verse, why was Christ made to be sin for us? How does that spiritual transaction occur?

Reflect
Which of the persons described in this lesson do you most readily identify with—the inner circle of three, Judas, or the rest of the Twelve? Why?

How can the examples of Peter and Judas prepare us for the challenges of serving the Savior? What have you learned from them that you can apply to your own life?

[15]So when they had eaten breakfast, Jesus said to Simon Peter, "Simon, son of Jonah, do you love Me more than these?" He said to Him, "Yes, Lord; You know that I love You." He said to him, "Feed My lambs." [16]He said to him again a second time, "Simon, son of Jonah, do you love Me?" He said to Him, "Yes, Lord; You know that I love You." He said to him, "Tend My sheep." [17]He said to him the third time, "Simon, son of Jonah, do you love Me?" Peter was grieved because He said to him the third time, "Do you love Me?" And he said to Him, "Lord, You know all things; You know that I love You." Jesus said to him, "Feed My sheep. [18]Most assuredly, I say to you, when you were younger, you girded yourself and walked where you wished; but when you are old, you will stretch out your hands, and another will gird you and carry you where you do not wish."
John 21:15-18

Christ's Enemies
In The Darkness

The enemies of Jesus also added to the suffering of Gethsemane. That may not surprise us. After all, that's what enemies do. Yet we must not take their actions for granted. These too were people for whom Christ was about to die. They also were people He dearly loved.

From about midnight until 8 in the morning, Jesus was made to stand before a succession of judges who allowed Him to be insulted and physically abused. Satan was probably hoping that this terrible treatment by the very people Jesus had come to save would convince Him to take an easier path than the cross. In any case, we can be sure Satan was happy about the added suffering all of this abuse was heaping on his hated antagonist.

Trials Before Annas, Caiaphas, And The Sanhedrin

Being brought before Annas (Jn. 18:13) was a glaring indignity. Annas was not a God-ordained high priest. He was not even a descendant of Aaron. He had gained the office by political intrigue. He had held the office from AD 6 to AD 15, and had passed it on to the members of his family. His son-in-law Caiaphas was now officially the high priest. But Annas was still in control, so much so that he is referred to as "high priest" in John 18:19. Annas treated Jesus with disdain, subjected Him to an illegal questioning process, and offered no objection when a temple guard rudely slapped Jesus across His face (vv.19-24).

Having bought enough time for the 71 members of the Sanhedrin to gather with Caiaphas, Annas sent Jesus on to a more official trial. The Sanhedrin was the Jewish Supreme Council. It was made up of chief priests, elders, and scribes who were experts in Jewish law. The presiding officer was the high priest.

Jesus was brought before this body of hostile men and subjected to the testimony of false witnesses. He had to watch Caiaphas' hypocritical show of piety as he tore his robes in a gesture of horror and screamed, "He has spoken blasphemy!" (Mt. 26:65). He had to hear the members of the Sanhedrin, who had gathered to carry out a plot instead of a fair trial, shout, "He is worthy of death" (v.66). He had to allow cruel guards to spit on His face, strike Him with their fists, and play their evil version of blindman's bluff by blindfolding Him, slapping Him, and challenging Him to tell them who did it (vv.67-68). But Jesus endured it all because He was determined to gain His objective—the salvation of the very sinners who were abusing Him.

Satan was able to increase the Lord's suffering on the way to the cross, but that was all he could accomplish.

Jesus knew from the Old Testament Scriptures that He would be treated this way. And all this mistreatment only strengthened His resolve. Satan was able to increase the Lord's suffering on the way to the cross, but that was all he could accomplish.

Trials Before Pilate And Herod

Although the Sanhedrin had already determined that Jesus should die, they met again early the next morning to make an official decision about how they would present the case to Pilate, the Roman governor of that region (Mk. 15:1; Lk. 22:2). The Sanhedrin had no power to execute anyone without permission from Rome (Jn. 18:31). So the guards led Jesus to Pilate, and the Jewish leaders presented their charges. At some point, Pilate announced his verdict: "I find no basis for a charge against this man" (Lk. 23:4). This enraged the conspirators. They declared that Jesus had begun in Galilee, and had spread His dangerous message throughout the entire region (v.5). Upon hearing that Jesus was a Galilean, Pilate saw a way out of the jam he was in. He sent Jesus to Herod Antipas, the Jewish ruler of that region. Maybe he could handle this problem.

Herod Antipas had been appointed by Rome to be the tetrarch of Galilee and Perea upon his father's death in 4 BC. He had, at the instigation of his wife Herodias, beheaded John the Baptist. A superstitious man, he had wanted to see Jesus to satisfy an inner fear that He might be John returned from the dead (Lk. 9:7-9). He plied Jesus with questions, but Jesus remained silent. At this, "Herod and his soldiers ridiculed and mocked Him. Dressing Him in an elegant robe, they sent Him back to Pilate" (23:11).

Pilate hated the Jewish leaders and was reluctant to order the crucifixion of Jesus. He again declared Christ's innocence (vv.14-15). In an effort to satisfy Jewish hostility, he ordered Jesus to be scourged. The whip used for this purpose consisted of several thongs loaded with pieces of metal. It tore chunks of flesh from the back of Jesus. Pilate then allowed his sadistic soldiers to indulge in mockery by pressing a crown of thorns onto the head of Jesus, dressing Him in royal purple, hailing Him as King of the Jews, and then paying homage to Him by striking Him in the face instead of kissing His cheek. Then he ordered Jesus brought out before the bloodthirsty throng and said, "Here is the man!" (Jn. 19:5). His probable meaning was, "Look at this poor fellow! How can He be a threat to anyone? Don't you think He has suffered enough?" But even seeing Jesus with a blood-soaked purple robe on His back and a crown of thorns on His head that sent streaks of blood coursing down His battered face evoked no pity. The response was, "Crucify! Crucify!" (v.6). Before long, Pilate gave in to the pressure and "handed Him over to them to be crucified" (v.16).

> **Before long, Pilate gave in to the pressure and "handed Him over to them to be crucified" (v.16).**

Jesus went out carrying the crossbeam on His bleeding shoulders, but it appears that He was so exhausted and weakened by the long night of abuse and the loss of blood from the scourging that He soon collapsed under its weight. The Roman soldiers compelled Simon, a Jew who had come all the way from Cyrene to celebrate the Passover, to carry the beam the rest of the way.

The Ridicule Of Onlookers

Seeing Jesus on the way to His crucifixion must have been an alarming experience for Satan, but he was not ready to acknowledge defeat. He continued in his efforts to heap upon Jesus all the pain and grief he could muster. He further tested the resolve of Jesus by inciting derisive taunts from the Jewish onlookers and the two criminals between whom He was crucified. Matthew wrote, "Those who passed by hurled insults at Him, shaking their heads and saying, 'You who are going to destroy the temple and build it in three days, save Yourself! Come down from the cross, if You are the Son of God!' In the same way the chief priests, the teachers of the law, and the elders mocked Him. 'He saved others,' they said, 'but He can't save Himself! He's the King of Israel! Let Him come down now from the cross, and we will believe in Him. He trusts in God. Let God rescue Him now if He wants Him, for He said, "I am the Son of God."' In the same way the robbers who were crucified with Him also heaped insults on Him" (27:39-44).

Satan undoubtedly hoped this challenge would be too much for Jesus to resist. Here He was, hanging on a cross in a weakened condition brought on by all He had gone through during the night and early morning hours. And yet His enemies were not satisfied!

In Gethsemane, Jesus had said that if He asked His Father, more than twelve legions of angels would be at His disposal (Mt. 26:53). The power to escape this dark hour was available to Him. But Jesus would not come down— He could not come down. Love held Him to the cross.

As in Gethsemane and during the trial, Satan was able to add to Jesus' pain. But he was unable to achieve his objective. He could not induce Him to bypass His appointment to die on the cross to pay the price of sin, break the power of death, and ensure final victory over the forces of evil.

STUDY
NO. **4**

Christ's Enemies In The Darkness

Matthew 26:53—"Do
you think that I cannot
now pray to My Father,
and He will provide Me
with more than twelve
legions of angels?"

Objective:
**To see how fallen
men contributed
to the sufferings
of Christ in
Gethsemane.**

Bible Memorization:
Matthew 26:53

Read:
**"Christ's Enemies
In The Darkness"
pp.30-33**

Warming Up

What kind of enemies have you encountered in your life? How has the knowledge of enemy opposition unsettled your thinking? How can it make you more determined?

Thinking Through

Who were Annas and Caiaphas? (pp.30-31). What does the involvement of the religious establishment say about the failures of human religion and its leaders?

Who were Herod and Pilate? (pp.31-32). How does their involvement in the execution of Jesus serve as an indictment of the Gentile world?

On page 33, we read about the crowd and its hateful ridicule of Christ. How was this part of Satan's attempts to derail the saving work of Christ?

Digging In
Key Text: Matthew 27:39-44

In our key text, three distinct groups of people mock Christ as He suffers on the cross. Who are they, and in what ways are their statements similar? How are they different?

Why do the religious leaders (vv.41-43) attack the character of Jesus' relationship with God the Father? Why do they attack His claim to be the Son of God?

What makes the mockery of the robbers so ironic? How does it reveal the darkness of the fallen human heart?

Going Further
Refer
Compare this lesson's memory verse with verse 40 of our key text. Why is it important to know that Jesus had options for escape, but refused to use them?

Reflect
On page 33, we read, "But Jesus would not come down—He could not come down. Love held Him to the cross." What does that statement say about the value God places on us? What is your response to such a great demonstration of love?

What have you learned about Christ's final hours in this study that might help you when facing trials? Facing enemies? Facing ridicule? In closing, spend a few moments thanking Christ for His love and asking for His help as you face the challenges of life.

[39]And those who passed by blasphemed Him, wagging their heads [40]and saying, "You who destroy the temple and build it in three days, save Yourself! If You are the Son of God, come down from the cross." [41]Likewise the chief priests also, mocking with the scribes and elders, said, [42]"He saved others; Himself He cannot save. If He is the King of Israel, let Him now come down from the cross, and we will believe Him. [43]He trusted in God; let Him deliver Him now if He will have Him; for He said, 'I am the Son of God.' [44]Even the robbers who were crucified with Him reviled Him with the same thing.
Matthew 27:39-44

Pushing Back The Darkness

In a very real sense, we can summarize Jesus' work on earth in one word—*victory*. He suffered in Gethsemane to push back the darkness we had brought on ourselves.

Suffering On The Cross As A Savior

While Jesus was hanging on the cross, He must have looked like a loser—a battered and bloody victim. Although He spoke agonizing words from the cross, He did not come down when He was challenged to do so. He remained nailed to a tree until the moment He died. He hung there as "the Savior of the world" (1 Jn. 4:14). He had been tempted and tested in every conceivable way, "yet was without sin" (Heb. 4:15).

Through His sinless life and miracles, Jesus had shown His mastery over the devil and all the forces of evil. He had tied up "the strong man" (Mt. 12:29). Yes, the devil is still a powerful enemy and has not conceded defeat, but he has been defeated. So when we submit to God and resist the devil we can put him to flight (Jas. 4:7).

Dying As A Conqueror

Jesus' final utterances from the cross were the words of a conqueror. After 3 hours of darkness, He triumphantly cried out, *tetelestai*, which means "It is finished." He knew He had suffered the desolation of hell and had emptied the cup of God's wrath against sin. He could now allow His spirit to depart from His body.

Paul declared that Jesus "canceled" the document that "was against us." Then he triumphantly added: "He took it away, nailing it to the cross. And having

36

disarmed the powers and authorities, He made a public spectacle of them, triumphing over them by the cross" (Col. 2:13-15).

Rising From The Dead As A Victor

Having won the victory over Satan by paying sin's penalty on the cross, Jesus proclaimed this victory by His resurrection. Because of His victory on the cross, "It was impossible for death to keep its hold on Him" (Acts 2:24). Death lost its "sting" (1 Cor. 15:55).

Ascending To Heaven As A Triumphant Intercessor

When Jesus ascended into heaven, He entered triumphantly and took His place of universal exaltation. He lives to intercede for us (Heb. 7:25). We who have been reconciled to God by trusting Jesus are guaranteed full and ultimate salvation "through His life" (Rom. 5:10).

**We wait confidently, knowing that
Jesus is already triumphant.**

We live in the interim between His ascension and His return. He is already reigning, but His rule is not yet fully manifested. One day every knee shall bow before Him and "every tongue confess that Jesus Christ is Lord, to the glory of God the Father" (Phil. 2:5-11). We wait confidently for that day, knowing that Jesus is already triumphant.

Who Killed Christ?

The Gospel accounts tell us that Jewish religious leaders rejected Jesus and pressured the Roman governor Pilate to have Him crucified. Recent reenactments of the suffering of Christ have renewed fears that if we look closely at who killed Christ we will stir up the flames of anti-Semitism.

The answer, however, is not to deny or ignore history, but to look carefully at the whole story. The fact is that Jesus Himself was the son of a Jewish mother and all of His apostles were Jewish, as were the great majority of His early followers.

His first followers were so Jewish that they actually resented the inclusion of Gentiles in the church as equals. Paul, the great apostle to the Gentiles, was proud of his Jewish heritage and joyfully pointed forward to the day when "all Israel will be saved" (Rom. 11:26).

We don't need to rewrite history. Bias against the Jewish people because of the actions of some of their ancestors is just as illogical as blaming all Christians for what some misguided followers of Jesus did in the Crusades. Or blaming all Germans for what the Nazis did!

Strictly speaking, Jesus was sentenced by Pilate, a Gentile governor. He was executed by Roman soldiers. Yet because of our own sins, all of us had a hand in killing Jesus as part of God's own plan to save us from our sins.

To receive and enjoy the eternal benefits of that salvation, we must believe and trust what He did for us on the cross (Jn. 3:16; Rom. 5:8-21).

Discovery Series Bible Study
Leader's And User's Guide

Statement Of Purpose

The *Discovery Series Bible Study* (DSBS) series provides assistance to pastors and leaders in discipling and teaching Christians through the use of RBC Ministries *Discovery Series* booklets. The DSBS series uses the inductive Bible-study method to help Christians understand the Bible more clearly.

Study Helps

Listed at the beginning of each study are the key verse, objective, and memorization verses. These will act as the compass and map for each study.

Some key Bible passages are printed out fully. This will help the students to focus on these passages and to examine and compare the Bible texts more easily—leading to a better understanding of their meanings. Serious students are encouraged to open their own Bible to examine the other Scriptures as well.

How To Use DSBS (for individuals and small groups)

Individuals—Personal Study

- Read the designated pages of the book.
- Carefully consider and answer all the questions.

Small Groups—Bible-Study Discussion

- To maximize the value of the time spent together, each member should do the lesson work prior to the group meeting.
- Recommended discussion time: 45–55 minutes.
- Engage the group in a discussion of the questions, seeking full participation from each of the members.

Overview Of Lessons

Study	Topic	Bible Text	Reading	Questions
1	Christ & God In Darkness	Matt. 26:38-44	pp.6-9	pp.10-11
2	Satan In The Darkness	Col. 2:13-15	pp.12-17	pp.18-19
3	Disciples In The Darkness	John 21:15-18	pp.21-27	pp.28-29
4	Enemies In The Darkness	Matt. 27:39-44	pp.30-33	pp.34-35

The DSBS format incorporates a "layered" approach to Bible study that includes four segments. These segments form a series of perspectives that become increasingly more personalized and focused. These segments are:

Warming Up. In this section, a general interest question is used to begin the discussion (in small groups) or "to get the juices flowing" (in personal study). It is intended to begin the process of interaction at the broadest, most general level.

Thinking Through. Here, the student or group is invited to interact with the *Discovery Series* material that has been read. In considering the information and implications of the booklet, these questions help to drive home the critical concepts of that portion of the booklet.

Digging In. Moving away from the *Discovery Series* material, this section isolates a key biblical text from the manuscript and engages the student or group in a brief inductive study of that passage of Scripture. This brings the authority of the Bible into the forefront of the study as we consider its message to our hearts and lives.

Going Further. This final segment contains two parts. In *Refer*, the student or group has the opportunity to test the ideas of the lesson against the rest of the Bible by cross-referencing the text with other verses. In *Reflect*, the student or group is challenged to personally apply the lesson by making a practical response to what has been learned.

Pulpit Sermon Series (for pastors and church leaders)

Although the *Discovery Series Bible Study* is primarily for personal and group study, pastors may want to use this material as the foundation for a series of messages on this important issue. The suggested topics and their corresponding texts are as follows:

Sermon No.	Topic	Text
1	Christ & God In The Darkness	Matt. 26:38-44
2	Satan In The Darkness	Col. 2:13-15
3	Christ's Disciples In The Darkness	John 21:15-18
4	Christ's Enemies In The Darkness	Matt. 27:39-44

Final Thoughts

The DSBS will provide an opportunity for growth and ministry. To internalize the spiritual truths of each study in a variety of environments, the material is arranged to allow for flexibility in the application of the truths discussed.

Whether DSBS is used in small-group Bible studies, adult Sunday school classes, adult Bible fellowships, men's and women's study groups, or church-wide applications, the key to the strength of the discussion will be found in the preparation of each participant. Likewise, the effectiveness of personal and pastoral use of this material will be directly related to the time committed to using this resource.

As you use, teach, or study this material, may you "grow in the grace and knowledge of our Lord and Savior Jesus Christ" (2 Pet. 3:18).

Reflections

OUR DAILY BREAD

Delivered right to your home!

You can make *Our Daily Bread* part of your regular time with God. Every month, you can receive a new booklet of devotional articles. Each day's topic is timely and lively and filled with wisdom and reliable instruction from God's Word.

To receive *Our Daily Bread* each month at home, just write to us at the address below or visit us at **www.odb.org/guide** to order online.

As part of the *Our Daily Bread* family, you'll also get opportunities to receive Bible-study guides and booklets on a variety of topics including creation, the church, and how to live the Christian life.

For program listings and other information about RBC resources, write to RBC Ministries at:

USA: PO Box 2222, Grand Rapids, MI 49501-2222
CANADA: Box 1622, Windsor, ON N9A 6Z7
RBC Web site: www.rbc.net